DAVID: GOD'S INSTRUMENT OF HORN

JOAN E. WATSON

David: God's Instrument of Horn Copyright ©2017 by Joan E. Watson.

All biblical quotations are from the Holy Bible, New King James Version®, Copyright © 1982 by Thomas Nelson, Inc. of the Bible unless otherwise noted.

All rights reserved.

Published by:
Instrument of Horn Ministries
P.O. Box 924203
Houston, Texas 77292
www.instrumentofhorn.org

Hardcover ISBN: 978-0-9990175-0-0

Paperback ISBN: 978-0-9990175-1-7

eBook ISBN: 978-0-9990175-2-4

Cover art by Marlon L. Adams II.
Cover design by Dana Pittman.
Interior text by Dana Pittman.

DEDICATION

I humbly dedicate this book to God the Father, God the Son, and God the Holy Spirit! Without their inspiration and guidance this work would not exist. I would like to thank my husband, David Sr., daughter Joan D., son David II., grandson Marlon II., for their patience, love, motivation, and encouragement, I pray that my love for you will always be felt and displayed!

I would like to also thank my Pastor Willie and Lady Ruth Collins of North Main COGIC, for developing, trusting, and allowing me to serve, teach, and preach God's Word. Thanks to all who prayed for the book to come forward.

In loving memory of my parents John and Thelma

Coleman, brother John Jr., grandson Breylon, and all my family members.

A tribute to my fourteen-year old cousin, Keondre Dillon Viser that lost his earthly battle to brain cancer on June 16, 2016, but received his eternal healing and crown in Heaven. Father, we curse the seed of cancer, the pain and grief it brings into the lives of so many, in Jesus' Name!

Cora Benjamin Coleman

April 11, 1895 - September 19, 1985

This book is lovingly dedicated to the cherished memories of an awesome woman. She was a phenomenal wife, a great mother, a committed grandmother, a friend, and a virtuous woman of God.

Mama, you lived a sanctified life before God and your family! I thank you for greatly assisting your youngest son, John F. Coleman, Sr., in raising his two motherless children, Joan and John, Jr. Mama, I am eternally appreciative! Mama, I will always love you!

For Marvel, memories of our Sisterhood will always be in my heart. Until we meet again...

CONTENTS

About David: God's Instrument of Horn	1
Illustration: Anonymous	3
Foreword	5
Preface	7
Poem: In Pursuit of Him	9
Introduction	11
1. David: The Shepherd	13
2. David: An Instrument of Horn	27
3. David: As a Friend	33
4. David: As a Father	49
5. David: As A Warrior/King	75
6. David: As A Worshipper/Psalmist	85
Poem: Image of You	109
I Offer Christ To You	111
Notes	113
About the Author	115
Contact Joan E. Watson	117
Join Ministry in The Word	119

David: God's Instrument of Horn, is a book that looks at the life of David of the Bible through a twenty-first century perspective. This book states the truth of God's Word line upon line, allowing the readers to insert themselves on the very scene of biblical history.

Travel with the author as she shares some of the many hats David wore on his journey through life. Readers of all ages and cultures should come away feeling the depth of David's love for Yahweh the God of Israel.

Each reader is invited to relax and feel the presence of the Holy Spirit in their reading experience.

ILLUSTRATION: ANONYMOUS

FOREWORD

Joan Watson is a blessed woman of God, divinely anointed and appointed by God to write this book, David: God's Instrument of Horn. It is important for God's people to read this message that God has given to her.

The story of David just happens to be one of my favorite biblical stories. Not only because David was a man "after God's own heart," but also because he was a man of faith and sincerity who revealed his deep love and understanding of God's law.

Joan captures the many sides of David in her book revealing him as a Shepherd, a Friend, a King, a Warrior, a Psalmist and an "Instrument of Horn."

When I first read her title, I did not understand it. As I began to read the book I still did not understand it until I read Chapter 2. That's when her message was revealed to me.

The main defenses of many beasts are their horns and therefore one could conclude that the horn is often a symbol of strength, honor, and dominion. As Joan explains in Chapter 2, the Lord exalted the horn of David and of his people.

I know Joan personally and I wholeheartedly support her Ministry. God has shown His approval of her work by allowing her message to come forth. This book is surely the result of hard work and many, many prayers. God commissioned us all to spread His Word, and through this book Joan is accomplishing that commission.

Ruth Collins
Executive Director of Women's Affairs
North Main Church, Houston, Texas

PREFACE

David, the son of Jesse, of the tribe of Judah, was born in Bethlehem. Bethlehem is also known as the "city of David." "Joseph also went up from Galilee, out of the city of Nazareth, into Judea, to the city of David, which is called Bethlehem, because he was of the house and lineage of David" (Luke 2:4).

Joshua, the son of Nun, led the children of Israel into the Promised Land after the death of Moses. Othniel, the son of Kenaz, was the first judge of Israel after Joshua's death. Israel's last judge was Samuel the prophet, the son of Elkanah. The children of Israel wanted a change in government and they insisted on a king. Saul the son of Kish was Israel's first king and he reigned as king several years. Saul's tenure as king displeased Yahweh exceedingly, leading to his kingship being rejected by Yahweh. Saul, as anointed king and leader refused to remain in the will of Yahweh; as a result, the kingdom was removed from him.

David, the son of Jesse was the successor to Saul, chosen by God as king of Israel. He was secretly anointed while Saul was still in power. David, returned to his father Jesse's house to receive this divine appointment, and was anointed by the prophet Samuel, who acted in obedience to the command of Yahweh. David eventually was in power as king of Judah and Israel. He is known as one Israel's greatest kings.

David was a man after God's own heart. Through life's ordeals, trials, and circumstances, he kept Yahweh as the true and living God in his heart. He is credited in the Book of Psalms as the writer of many of the prayers, songs, and psalms. His character, personality, and life events are clearly recognizable in many of the psalms. He was a worshipper; he worshipped Yahweh in spirit and in truth.

Father, let your children always have a tender and repentant heart toward You, earnestly giving You all the love, honor, praise, and worship You majestically deserves.

POEM: IN PURSUIT OF HIM

BY JOAN E. WATSON

Taking this journey pursuing Him,
My expectations are never dim.
Anticipating what I will discover and learn,
Creates excitement that I strongly yearn.
As He lovingly guides, assuredly I will pursue,
Committed to reaching a pinnacle, I will utilize every clue.
When He apprehends me with His passionate might,
I will relinquish my quest ceasing the flight.
In His presence, there is great beauty and awe,
Basking closely in His radiance I will continually draw!

INTRODUCTION

What makes David one of the Bible's most discussed characters? He was an anointed, gifted, and humbled individual, who wore many helmets during his lifetime. Most of the roles he played were outstanding; a few on the other hand were dishonorable. This book will discuss David's life as a shepherd, an instrument of horn, a friend, a father, a warrior/king, and a worshipper/psalmist. The Holy Spirit's presence upon him and his role as friend, father, warrior/king, and worshipper/psalmist will be explored in depth.

David was a multifaceted individual who knew how to appeal to Yahweh to accomplish various goals and assignments in his life. At an early age, it is apparent that he developed an intimate relationship with Yahweh, and maintained a Yahweh-centered focus in almost every phase of his life. David, whose name is known to anyone who has read the Bible, was not flawless. However, even with his imperfections, he was still a man after God's own heart, not because he was sinless; but because God saw David's obedience. God was so impressed with his willingness to obey that he allowed His only begotten son, Jesus of Nazareth, to be born of the seed of David according to the flesh.

Godly obedience will help one navigate through presumptuous thinking. Submissiveness to God's authority is the incubation process one will undergo while waiting for the revelation of God's perfect will. David's commitment, faith, humility, love, and obedience toward God contributed to the perpetual establishment of the throne. His lineage and throne is the one from which Jesus Christ the King of Kings will reign in Israel forever. "He will be great, and will be called the Son of the Highest; and the Lord God will give Him the throne of His father David. And He will reign over the house of Jacob forever, and of His kingdom there will be no end" (Luke 1:32-33).

1

DAVID: THE SHEPHERD

DAVID, a descendant of Ruth of Moab and Boaz of Bethlehem, was the eighth son of Jesse of Bethlehem, Judea. "Now David was the son of that Ephrathite of Bethlehem Judah, whose name was Jesse, and who had eight sons. And the man was old, advanced in years, in the days of Saul" (I Samuel 17:12).

David undoubtedly was a faithful and obedient son to Jesse his father. He was entrusted to look after Jesse's sheep, and it was important to his father that the sheep be cared for properly. He realized that taking exceptional care of the flock of sheep would keep his relationship with his father pleasing.

Scripture documents that David's first occupation was that of a shepherd. "And Samuel said to Jesse,

Are all the young men here? Then he said, There remains yet the youngest, and there he is, keeping the sheep, And Samuel said to Jesse, Send and bring him. For we will not sit down till he comes here" (I Samuel 16:11). The occupation of a shepherd was a common one among the Israelites. Sheep were used for essentials such as clothing, food, milk, and animal sacrifices, and much more. David's job as a shepherd included protecting the sheep from vicious predators as well as leading them to green pastures and drinking water. At the end of a workday the shepherd's job did not end; he was on call always to secure the safety of the flock.

It was very important to continually keep a watchful eye out for the sheep. If any of the flock wandered away from the fold, it was a major cause for concern. The shepherd would have to temporarily leave the rest of the sheep, to search out the sheep that had strayed away from the group. Each sheep had to be counted upon their return to the fold, and an accurate headcount had to be maintained. The shepherd had to have a keen instinct, as well as a keen sense of sight and sound, while the sheep were in his or her care. Though sheep usually stay in groups of four or five, and adjust well with other sheep, they are no match in fighting off or protecting themselves from wolves, coyotes, lions, bears, or other wild animals.

Shepherds had to be dedicated to the sheep that they were expected to protect, provide for, and preserve life to the best of their ability. Good leadership is vital in the role of the shepherd; one must cautiously lead the sheep, not forcibly drive them into fertile pastures. The shepherd has a close relationship with the sheep, so they can easily know and recognize their shepherd's voice. It is important for the shepherd to provide maximum security to the sheep always.

David, an obedient son to his father Jesse, and a good shepherd, would not be found playing in the fields, pastures, or caves. Reflecting upon the father-son relationship of Jesse and David, I am reminded of God the Father and Jesus's intimate bond. The father-son relationship in both scenarios is one of unity and they were in one accord even in each other's absence. Although Jesse was not with David as he nurtured the sheep, he operated as obediently as though his father was present. If Jesse sought David to come home or to send him a message, Jesse or the messenger would not have to play a guessing game to discover his whereabouts. He would be in an expected area doing his expected assignment of caring for the flock.

David, like Jesus, was submissive and obedient to

his father. Jesus, during His earthly ministry, never tried to promote His own agenda. Everything Jesus performed on earth during His ministry was accommodative and reflective toward His Father. Jesus was observant to execute all assignments given Him by His Father to completion. Jesus's goal was to satisfy and please His Father in all that He would say and do. "Then Jesus answered and said to them, Most assuredly, I say to you, the Son can do nothing of Himself, but what He sees the Father do; for whatever He does, the Son also does in like manner" (John 5:19). It is so crucial for earthly fathers to do their best as parents, their children are watching!

When relationships natural or spiritual are intimately woven and respected, one can clearly see how all parties can be completely in sync with one other. David and his father, Jesse, were normally at different places, but David understood the importance of the directives and goals he had to attain and maintain in honor of his father wherever he was. Jesus left eternity by divine proclamation and entered time, transitioning into the natural from the supernatural and continually obeying the will of His Father Yahweh and his earthly parents. "Jesus said to them, Most assuredly, I say to you, before Abraham was, I Am" (John 8:58).

DAVID: GOD'S INSTRUMENT OF HORN

David, like Jesus, at a very young age devoted his life to the things of God. He had a great deal of alone time while caring for his father's flock. He entertained himself and the sheep by playing his instrument and fellowshipping with Yahweh. While children of Jesus's age were probably playing with their siblings or friends and enjoying different pastimes, Jesus was found pursuing the things of God. "His parents went to Jerusalem every year at the Feast of the Passover. And when He was twelve years old, they went up to Jerusalem according to the custom of the feast. When they had finished the days, as they returned, the Boy Jesus lingered behind in Jerusalem. And Joseph and His mother did not know it; but supposing Him to have been in the company, they went a day's journey, and sought Him among their relatives and acquaintances. So when they did not find Him, they returned to Jerusalem, seeking Him. Now so it was that after three days they found Him in the temple, sitting in the midst of the teachers, both listening to them and asking them questions. And all who heard Him were astonished at His understanding and answers. So when they saw Him, they were amazed; and His mother said to Him, Son, why have You done this to us? Your father and I have sought You anxiously. And He said to them, Why did you seek Me? Did you not know that

I must be about My Father's business? But they did not understand the statement which He spoke to them. Then He went down with them and came to Nazareth, and was subject to them, but His mother kept all these things in her heart" (Luke 2:41-51). The profound statement that Jesus made to His earthly parents must have been a blow to them. Had Jesus been told that Joseph was not His biological father? Jesus's divinity never diminished in humanity. Being truly God and truly man, He is omniscient, all-knowing.

In His work, too, Jesus, like David, spent a lot of time alone in the fields with His (human) sheep. Jesus could have spent most of His time in the synagogue with the religious leaders, or just casually hanging out with others with no specific agenda. Instead, during His ministry, He devoted a great deal of time developing the sheep, His Father's sheep, that were given to Him. "And seeing the multitudes, He went up on a mountain, and when He was seated His disciples came to Him. Then he opened His mouth and taught them, saying:" (Matthew 5:1-2). Jesus managed His time wisely on earth to feed His sheep spiritual food that would sustain them throughout life's journey. Jesus, like David, sought God in prayer concerning various areas of His administration. "And when He had sent the multitudes away, He went up on the mountain by Himself to pray. Now when evening came, he was alone there" (Matthew 14:23). Jesus spent time in solitude to communicate with Yahweh His Father in prayer concerning His will. Fellowshipping with others is important, quiet time with God is essential!

Jesus: The Good Shepherd
"I am the good shepherd. The good shepherd gives His life for the sheep."
John 10:11

The Israelites had adopted the customs of the other nations when they requested a king. God had given the prophet Samuel, Israel's last judge, the commission of anointing Saul as Israel's first king. Since the people wanted a king God allowed them to have one. After the people confirmed Saul as their king, he reigned for several years. Samuel the prophet went to King Saul to give him instructions from God. Saul was told by Samuel to go and destroy the Amalekites and everything there. "Now go and attack Amalek, and utterly destroy all that they have, and do not spare them. But kill both man and woman, infant and nursing child, ox and sheep, camel and donkey" (I Samuel 15:3).

Saul and his army went after the Amalekites and slaughtered the people but refused to kill King Agag and the best of their livestock. Saul planned in his heart that he was going to do things the way he wanted to do them, not the way God had commanded. Saul's disobedience caused God to know that He could not trust Saul to lead His people. God alerted the prophet Samuel of Saul's conduct. "I greatly regret that I have set up Saul as king, for he has turned back from following Me, and has not performed My commandments. And it grieved Samuel, and he cried out to the LORD all night" (I Samuel 15:11).

Can God trust us to do what we have been anointed and ordained to do? Or will we walk in the spirit of Saul, and do things according to the lust of the flesh, the lust of the eyes, and the pride of life? When Saul allowed disobedience of God's Word and command to dominate him, there was a spiritual breakdown in the kingship. God had bestowed on Saul a great honor as the first king of His chosen people, Israel. Yet, Saul allowed pride and self-centeredness to cloud his judgment, failing to realize that he was subject to the greatest King of all subjects, also known as Yahweh. He failed to appreciate that obedience was a requirement to maintain his position in leadership. He was informed by Samuel, the prophet, that because he did not follow the instructions that God had given him he would not be allowed to continue ruling as king of Israel. "For rebellion is as the sin of witchcraft, And stubbornness is as iniquity and idolatry. Because you have rejected the word of the LORD, He also has rejected you from being king" (I Samuel 15:23).

"But now your kingdom shall not continue. The LORD has sought for Himself a man after His own heart, and the LORD has commanded him to be commander over His people, because you have not kept what the LORD commanded you" (I Samuel 13:14). David of the tribe of Judah, son of Jesse of Bethlehem, the youngest of Jesse's sons, was anointed by the prophet Samuel to be King of Israel. He was the least likely candidate of Jesse's sons to be considered eligible by man's standard to attain the kingship of Israel, which was a political and a divine appointment. David was anointed to replace the rejected King Saul, the son of Kish a Benjamite, who allowed pride, greed, and public opinion to take precedence over obedience and faithfulness to the LORD. Will we allow popularity and acceptance by man to overshadow God's purpose?

David was declared by God to be a man after His own heart. God knew David before he was a thought in his parent's minds. He was known by God before he was contoured in his mother's warm silhouette. Just as David was known by the LORD, so are we all known by the Author and Finisher. Yahweh is from everlasting to everlasting; He is omnipotent, omniscient, and omnipresent. He is the Ancient of Days. Does the knowledge God have of us grieve Him or please Him?

God, who is mankind's brilliant playwright, brings His creation to His calculated and predestined stage of life, in His designated time and season. David, like all humans, had to ad-lib an unknown script which must be acted out with each performance that God allows to be played. He, like others, is not afforded a dress rehearsal before God's declaration is pronounced concerning the cycles of their life. Before David was circumcised on the eighth day and weaned from his mother's breast milk, he was seen by God as a man after His own heart. When David was a boy spending his days and nights on the Judean hills keeping his father's sheep, God saw him as a man after His own heart. Even when he was immersed in human flaws, God still saw him as a man after His own heart.

When Yahweh stated to Samuel that David was a man after His own heart, he was still a young boy. However, when God speaks or declares something He sees the end of it and pronounces with clarity the outcome or conclusions. "Declaring the end from the beginning, And from ancient times things that are not yet done, Saying My counsel shall stand, And I will do all My pleasure" (Isaiah 46:10).

The heart is an intricate part of our being; it has massive capabilities to love or to hate. It can be indifferent, or even numb to events that occur in and around our lives. The heart has a mechanism in it to reciprocate, ignore, perceive, receive, reject, ponder, or duplicate the messages that come in and out of it. These messages or feelings can be real, false, stimulating, or they can be coded with chaos. When an individual chooses to remove all barriers, enclosures, and gated blockages from around their heart and allow the love of God to permeate its very texture, awesome feelings can flood one's entire being. David allowed his heart to reciprocate God's love and he willingly exchanged his stony heart for a heart of flesh. When this transaction is done in the realm of the spirit, intimacy takes place and the core expands outwardly absorbing like a sponge the love of God. David had a heart that was tender in worship, praise, humility, obedience, and adoration to a Holy and Majestic Creator.

Reflecting on the Word of God in the Book of Jeremiah, God talks to Jeremiah, calling him by his name and sharing some prophetic dialogue with him. He is in direct conversation with Yahweh. Jeremiah insistently tells Yahweh that he is a child; this leads one to think that Jeremiah thought the task was much too great for him because he was young. Yahweh commands him in their conversation not to say that he is a child. "Then the word of the Lord came to me, saying: Before I formed you in the womb I knew you; Before you were born I sanctified you; I ordained you a prophet to the nations. Then said I: Ah LORD God! Behold, I cannot speak, for I am a youth. But the LORD said to me: Do not say, I am a youth, For you shall go to all to whom I send you, And whatever I command you, you shall speak" (Jeremiah 1:4-7). This is a great example of how God declares the end from the beginning. God sees the final product and focuses not on the seed but much more on the cultivated and matured fruit.

As a young boy tending his father's flock, David had a lot of time to spend before the LORD and meditate on His statutes and precepts. Certainly, when the sheep had grazed, drunk water, and frolicked, they too wanted to relax. As David rested when the sheep did, he could pray and talk to Yahweh. Surely the sheep bleating all day gave him the desire to be still and talk to Yahweh. Since his mind was not occupied with things going on at home or in the neighborhood he was able to concentrate on things above. He was in a perfect environment to receive one-on-one uninterrupted download from Yahweh.

Being called a man after God's own heart did not exempt him from human weakness and a sinful life; it merely insulated the purpose and calling God had on David's life. God can see the predominant intent and motive one embraces, whereas others can only see the outward signs. God operates by faith: His statement to Samuel the prophet about David being "a man after His own heart" was a faith declaration. "By faith we understand that the worlds were framed by the word of God, so that the things which are seen were not made of things which are visible" (Hebrews 11:3).

God did not have to use nails, hammers, saws, cement, bricks, elbow grease, Play-Doh, magic, witchcraft, etc., to form anything in creation, He simply spoke by faith and it was! "Then God said, Let there be light; and there was light" (Genesis 1:3).

What an awesome Father! Who in their right mind would not allow a powerful and loving Father to escort them into an eternal Heaven? Who in their right mind would forfeit an opportunity to be eternally surrounded and submerged in perfect love and peace.

2

DAVID: AN INSTRUMENT OF HORN

DAVID IS AN "INSTRUMENT OF HORN,"[1] anointed and called by God to be Israel's second king. Being God's Instrument, David showed valor as a boy attending his father's sheep. God's mighty spiritual hands were there to help, assist, and strengthen as David killed the bear and the lion. David was exclusively used by God to usher in the tribe of Judah to reign in Israel. This reign will culminate with Jesus sitting on the throne perpetually. "There I will make the horn of David grow; I will prepare a lamp for My Anointed" (Psalm 132:17). God promises growth and exaltation for them that have power and uses it for His glory, more will be given. God promises that David's throne will continue forever, leading to Jesus the Light of the World!

David displayed a great amount of strength from youth until full maturity. His faith was very great toward Yahweh, and his testimonies served as a reminder of God's faithfulness. He had seen God's strength in fighting his battles. He walked in faith in his relationship with God. A striking example occurred when David was on an assignment given to him by his father to deliver food to his brothers. While there he observed a serious situation concerning Goliath the giant and Israel's army, and he volunteered to eliminate Goliath, Israel's enemy. King Saul, being concerned about his youth and inexperience in war, was very reluctant to grant him permission to fight Goliath. "Then David said to Saul, "Let no man's heart fail because of him: your servant will go and fight with this Philistine. And Saul said to David, You are not able to go against this Philistine to fight with him; for you are a youth, and he a man of war from his youth" (I Samuel 17:32-33).

David, recognizing King Saul's lack of trust in his ability to compete in battle with Goliath, offered a vivid testimony to King Saul. "But David said to Saul, Your servant used to keep his father's sheep, and when a lion or a bear came and took a lamb out of the flock, I went out after it and struck it, and delivered the lamb from its mouth: and when it arose against me, I caught it by its beard, and struck and killed it. Your servant has killed both lion and bear: and this uncircumcised Philistine will be like one of them, seeing he has defied the armies of the living God" (I Samuel 17:34-36). Instantly, David gave King Saul an oral resume of his work experience as a shepherd in Bethlehem, Judea. He was boldly proclaiming and glorifying God as his Jehovah-Nissi (Banner), Jehovah-Jireh (Provider), and his Jehovah-Rohi (Shepherd), to the king.

David, in his attempt to declare the favor of God upon his life, advised King Saul that God was his divine protector. Whether it be man or beast, God is all powerful against any foe or element that would try to challenge him. He gave the king additional facts about how God had vindicated him in dangerous trials. "Moreover David said, The LORD, who delivered me from the paw of the lion and from the paw of the bear, He will deliver me from the hand of this Philistine. And Saul said to David, Go, and the LORD be with you" (I Samuel 17:37). David's persistence prevailed, and King Saul agreed to let him fight Goliath, Israel's enemy.

King Saul knew that Goliath had won many battles from his youth until the present; he could not begin to imagine how David in his youth, even with

God's help, could be equally successful. David stood as a giant on the faithfulness of God, declaring to King Saul that Yahweh, the same God that raised him from amongst his kinsman to become Israel's first king, would be able to lift him up victoriously against God's enemy Goliath, the uncircumcised Philistine.

David was not fearful or ashamed to publicly announce how the LORD had showed him kindness. He was appreciative of God's tenderness and faithfulness to him in times of trouble and danger. His faith in God was so great that it didn't matter if he was ridiculed and mocked before others. He stood on what he knew to be factual, regardless of unbelief, scrutiny, and sarcasm. His childlike faith early in his life pleased God. It showed God and others his humility and the complete trust he had in Yahweh. God wants us to walk in faith toward Him and not fear what giant-like obstacles can do to us. "But without faith it is impossible to please Him, for he who comes to God must believe that He is, and that He is a rewarder of those who diligently seek Him" (Hebrews 11:6).

This childlike faith that David possessed is what we should all have in our relationship with our Father. It is good for all of us to see through the eyes of a child the presence of God in our lives. Children trust adults to do exactly what they tell them they will do.

Children do not allow doubt and disbelief to cloud their faith and hope about something they believe will happen. "Assuredly, I say to you, whoever does not receive the kingdom of God as a little child will by no means enter it" (Luke 18:17).

David's keen perception and trust in God's ability allowed him to walk in confidence knowing that God would prevail. He had the awesome experience of witnessing God's power to protect him and the sheep, while he was caring for the flock. When his natural father was not there to defend and assist him amid imminent danger, Yahweh was always there. "When my father and my mother forsake me, then the LORD will take care of me" (Psalm 27:10). David vocally made it known to the king that it was not his strength or might; it all belonged to the power of God. He was convinced by repeated victories that nothing was too hard for Yahweh! Are you willing to give God all of His glory? Will you depend on the power and might of Yahweh to bring you through life's storms and adversities?

3

DAVID: AS A FRIEND

During one's life people enter and exit for various reasons. Some relationships are short term or medium term and others are long term. When using the words short, medium or long, thoughts are primarily on the depth or volume of the friendship more than on chronological length. Some friendships are just friendly episodes in the lives of others, having no reference. Other friendships may endure for a longer time but prove not to be solid and sincere throughout their duration. Few friendships last a life cycle and beyond. The ones that endures are built on a foundation of love, trust, honesty, value, worth, and agape love. David and Jonathan's friendship is a perfect example.

David the son of Jesse became a common name to

King Saul and his household. The king arrived at a decision to use David to defeat the giant Goliath, and later used his musical gift to soothe his episodes of delusions. David was eventually promoted in the kingdom and became King Saul's armor bearer. During his service to the king he became a dear friend of Jonathan the son of the king.

David and Jonathan bonded strongly and their friendship grew to be one they both cherished. Their friendship, like true friendships, were built primarily on trust and respect. Trust is a necessary ingredient for any personal relationship, to survive. Jonathan and David both possessed an obedient spirit toward their fathers. Jonathan served his father, the king of Israel, in a military capacity. Jonathan, like David, loved Yahweh; their spiritual bond was strong enough to sustain the diverse degrees of conflict that life often brings. David and Jonathan both were courageous men who were not intimidated by war or the appearance of war. They shared many common attributes; however, the love for God surpassed all commonalities.

David and Jonathan were true friends. When King Saul openly opposed David, Jonathan did not allow his father's feelings to snuff out his friendship and love toward David. Jonathan and David remained constant and devoted to each other even during intense danger. This unique type of friendship goes past the human propensity to love, and it incorporates the divine nature of love. The love that David and Jonathan exhibited toward each other is agape love. This type of love is what Jesus always demonstrates to His Body. Can we sincerely love others to this magnitude without allowing envy, strife, offense, and the toxin of unforgiveness to take root?

Jonathan and David led separate lives, yet they had the time and desire to go outside their sphere, embracing each other in a brotherly friendship. "to know the love of Christ which passes knowledge; that you may be filled with all the fullness of God" (Ephesians 3:19). This unique friendship that David and Jonathan possessed surpasses mankind's finite ability to love, and incorporates God's infinite capability to love. When the human ability to love, yield, forgive, trust, and believe each other diminishes, know that God's power source of love, peace, faith, and compassion, perseveres. David and Jonathan's friendship was a great example of unconditional love.

Jonathan did not think more highly of himself than he ought just because his father was the king of Israel. He allowed the personality and character traits of David to be a building block toward a long-term or lifetime friendship. David did not permit the attempts King Saul made on his life to shatter his commitment to be a true friend to Jonathan. He stared past the biological DNA in King Saul and Jonathan, and he chose to embrace the spiritual DNA between himself and Jonathan in God. David and Jonathan's unconditional love for each other prevailed no matter what opposition came their way!

"Then David fled from Naioth in Ramah, and went and said to Jonathan, What have I done? What is my iniquity, and what is my sin before your father, that he seeks my life" (I Samuel 20:1)? This passage from scripture reflects the time when David fled from King Saul, and the king sought to find David. David arrived at a decision to leave and seek guidance from Jonathan concerning the dilemma he had about King Saul. Trust and loyalty toward each other allowed David the confidence to seek Jonathan about this urgency, knowing he would not be disappointed.

"So Jonathan said to David, Whatever you yourself desire, I will do it for you. And David said to Jonathan, Indeed tomorrow is the New Moon, and I should not fail to sit with the king to eat. But let me go, that I may hide in the field until the third day at evening" (I Samuel 20:4-5). Jonathan responded to David's pleas by telling him "Whatsoever." Whatsoever denotes endless requests granted within the power of the person's capability to do so. The powerful Yahweh fills this description completely. "And God said to Moses, I AM WHO I AM" (Exodus 3:14a). Jonathan extended agape love to David. Jonathan was simply saying to David Consider it done, friend. Do we love our family, friends, neighbors, and others to this extent, to maintain a "whatsoever" relationship?

"So, Jonathan made a covenant with the house of David, saying, Let the LORD require it at the hand of David's enemies. Now Jonathan again caused David to vow, because he loved him: for he loved him as he loved his own soul" (I Samuel 20:16-17). The covenant that Jonathan made was not with David alone, but with David's family also. Jonathan requested a promise of David, that he would show kindness to his family forever. A friendship speaks volumes when it's able to extend itself generationally. It is wise to recognize God's favor and anointing on the lives of family and friends, and then to embrace who God embraces.

"Then Jonathan said to David, Go in peace, since we have both sworn in the name of the LORD, saying, May the LORD be between you and me, and between your descendants and my descendants, forever. So he arose and departed, and Jonathan went into the city" (I Samuel 20:42). This renewed covenant was a promise to show kindness to Jonathan's family forever. David could depend on Jonathan to follow through on requests and vice versa. Jonathan's and David's faith in Yahweh was deeper than in each other; they both had faith in an unseen God and all His works. They could easily befriend each other because they were both connected and shared the love of Yahweh and the Holy Spirit. Jonathan and David were both warriors for the Nation of Israel, and they demonstrated their faith in Yahweh through their dependence on God to win battles on their behalf. Their relationship in serving the God of Israel was important to both and they were not ashamed to display that love.

David and Jonathan chose to be friends one with the other, allowing their friendship to grow in love and confidence at an unlimited pace. Real friendship does not weigh the flaws or blemishes of the other; it looks directly at the content and basis of the heart. Jonathan and David's friendship was as close as or closer than that between biological brothers. Each one of them had male siblings; however, the bible does not make any mention of a deep friendship between them. "Greater love has no one than this, than to lay down one's life for his friends" (John 15:13). Jonathan was committed to Yahweh, his earthly father, and to David. David was committed to Yahweh, his earthly father, and to Jonathan.

During their lives, there were times when both were in obvious danger while in the presence of King Saul. "Then Saul sought to pin David to the wall with the spear, but he slipped away from Saul's presence; and he drove the spear into the wall. So David fled and escaped that night. Saul also sent messengers to David's house to watch him and to kill him in the morning. And Michal, David's wife, told him, saying, If you do not save your life tonight, tomorrow you will be killed" (I Samuel 19:10-11). King Saul had allowed rage and anger to fill his heart concerning David to the point that he wanted David's life immediately. He knew that Yahweh had rejected his kingship and had approved David to be the second king of Israel. King Saul did not take this rejection well and he retaliated against David, by transferring his own deficiencies and disobedience toward him.

Jonathan faced an attack on his life by his own father, King Saul, because of his close friendship with David. Saul seemingly felt that Jonathan had dealt deceitfully with him concerning David. David had demonstrated obedience and loyalty while serving

King Saul and the king had no legitimate reason to be at odds with him. When Jonathan inquired of his father, why he wanted to kill David and what had he done to make him so angry, the king immediately was riled up against Jonathan. This question evidently stirred up a hornet's nest in the pit of Saul's heart. "Then Saul cast a spear at him to kill him, by which Jonathan knew that it was determined by his father to kill David" (I Samuel 20:33). This incident made Jonathan understand there was no convincing the king to give up his pursuit of taking David's life. Jonathan could see that his father's adamant mindset was to destroy David's very existence. During this phase of Saul's life, one can clearly see the absence of devotion and fellowship with Yahweh on his part. Saul had allowed his hatred to cloud an intimate and worship-filled relationship with Yahweh.

Jonathan's and David's devoted friendship withstood the perils of King Saul, who was a menace to them. They continued to regard each other with high esteem and respect despite conflict and opposition. King Saul would travel in and out of his episodes of paranoia, which would be directed primarily toward David. Obviously, the king could control his levels of delusion he displayed and who he would direct them toward. Of all the different ranks, personalities and people who surrounded him on a day-to-day basis in Israel, the Bible only gives the names of Jonathan and David as being openly targeted by King Saul. He had allowed pride to invade his spirit and he no longer walked in humility with Yahweh or with others.

Within the span of their friendship, David and Jonathan, maintained a love for Yahweh. The love that they shared with God enabled them to be transparent with each other, allowing Yahweh's love to be a reflection upon their friendship which in turn gave God the glory! Although Jonathan and the servants were given the directive to kill David, Jonathan chose to walk in agape love toward David, utterly disobeying the king and honorably obeying the LORD. Jonathan loved and honored his earthly father, but he loved Yahweh and His commandments and statues much more. Can our Heavenly Father trust us to love Him more than anyone or anything?

Jonathan and David remained true friends and the favor of God was on their lives. They continually enjoyed each other friendship, trusting in Yahweh during every phase of their relationship. Saul knew that David was chosen and called by God. David's stellar character always radiated when he was given an assignment by the king. He continued to be exemplary in his role as a servant.

While playing his instrument for Saul to soothe him from the evil tormenting spirits, King Saul tried to kill him with the javelin. David, having escaped on two occasions from King Saul, knew for sure that Yahweh was with him and not with Saul. "And he said, Please let me go, for our family has a sacrifice in the city, and my brother has commanded me to be there. And now, please let me get away and see my brothers. Therefore he has not come to the king's table" (I Samuel 20:29). King Saul's passion to kill David increased throughout his tenure as king and his hatred and hostility toward him continued to intensify. Life is to be lived and loved, not lived and doomed!

David and Jonathan had a strong bond of friendship where only death could access the pause button. They were separated in life only because of the anxiety and drama that King Saul allowed to be his crown. David, unfortunately became a fugitive on the run from King Saul. Jonathan made a final attempt to comfort his friend and to have him console him as well, before they departed from each other. "As soon as the lad had gone, David arose from a place toward the south, fell on his face to the ground, and bowed down three times. And they kissed one another; and they wept together, but David more so" (I Samuel 20:41).

The separation of David from Jonathan was excruciating. Reality was now visible to David – he knew he had to leave behind all the tangibles that he loved. He had to leave his wife, Michal who is also the king's daughter, his friend, Jonathan the king's son, the altar of Yahweh, his family and friends, and everything. Imagine having to be disrupted from one's family, country, culture, comfort, and the worship of God and driven away to a strange land and their strange gods.

Saul had given his daughter, Michal to be David's wife and they agreed with the marriage. King Saul had initially told him that his oldest daughter Merab could be his wife if he fought on the battlefield for the LORD. David did agree to fight the battle against the Philistines and he was triumphant in battle. This was not what the king expected! Saul intentions for David to marry his oldest daughter were not sincere; he just wanted to use her as bait to lure him to his early death. King Saul decided in his restricted and confused mind that this was the battle that would eliminate David from the face of the earth. When David returned to get his bride-to-be, Merab, she had already been given to another by the name of Adriel to marry. With Merab promised to Adriel, King Saul offered his youngest daughter, Michal, to David as a replacement. King Saul was attempting to play some ungodly and unfruitful mind game with him.

"Then Saul said to David, Here is my older daughter Merab; I will give her to you as a wife. Only be valiant for me, and fight the LORD'S battles. For Saul thought, Let my hand not be against him, but let the hand of the Philistines be against him. So David said to Saul, Who am I, and what is my life or my father's family in Israel, that I should be son-in-law to the king? But it happened at the time when Merab, Saul's daughter, should have been given to David, that she was given to Adriel the Meholathite as a wife. Now Michal, Saul's daughter loved David. And they told Saul, and the thing pleased him. So Saul said, I will give her to him, that she may be a snare to him, and that the hand of the Philistines may be against him. Therefore Saul said to David a second time, You shall be my son-in-law today" (I Samuel 18:17-21).

King Saul's intentions concerning David were not honest and sincere – but hatred-filled and demeaning. King Saul of course had yet another hidden agenda in giving David his other daughter, Michal, to become his wife. I am sure David, a shepherd boy with no substantial backing of his own, did not have much income or property to bring to the marriage, he was probably honored by King Saul's offer. There is speculation whether David perceived the obvious deception and trickery in the king's intents and motives. King Saul came up with the idea of David killing one hundred Philistines and bringing their foreskins as proof to him, as a requirement for his marriage to Michal. King Saul really believed in his scarred mind that David would be incapable of accomplishing this heroic attainment. He, not only surpassed the one hundred foreskins but also went the extra step and delivered two hundred Philistines' foreskins, twice as many as were required. This great achievement forced King Saul to release Michal in marriage to David; finally agreeing to the marriage to save his image.

I am reminded via later scripture of how David was treated by King Saul. When Jesus was teaching the Sermon on the Mount of Olives, He gave these infamous words, "But I tell you not to resist an evil person. But whoever slaps you on your right cheek, turn the other to him also" (Matthew 5:39). David regardless of life's events, continued his purposeful journey. Although he could have allowed his flesh to supersede God's divine will and purpose for his life, he refused to operate in carnality concerning his destiny. David believed the Word of God given by the prophet Samuel to him. He had time to reflect on the anointing of oil that was ministered to him in the presence of his family by Samuel the Prophet. David had to remain submissive, humble, and obedient to the Father, as he allowed the timing of his appointment to be manifested.

David was careful not to leap before the manifestation concerning the purpose God ordained for his life. One step and timing is a necessary tool to achieve divine destiny.[2] Pondering on great biblical highlights, I reflect on Moses and the children of Israel leaving Egypt. If Moses did not have the faith to walk in the direction that God was leading him, the timing of the miracle could have been aborted. If Moses had allowed the magnitude of the Red Sea to prevent him from moving forward, he could have extended the Israelites' stay in Egypt. Similarly, David had faith, and realized that his purpose exceeded the depravity of King Saul's mind. Moses' obedience allowed him and the Nation of Israel to escape the steel jaws of Egyptian slavery. The elevated values that David displayed are excellent character traits; they are essential for great leaders and great relationships.

David did not want to misuse or abuse the anointing as the next king of Israel. He knew how to submit well to authority. He did not let his eagerness to become king outweigh the tenure of King Saul, God's first appointee as king of Israel. David realized if Yahweh allowed the controversies to occur in his life, He was working for a good resolution. He chose not to allow selfishness to override divine providence. Will you get in a hurry after the prophecy is given and take a short cut, or will you choose the scenic route prior to the manifestation?

4

DAVID: AS A FATHER

DAVID, was the father of many children by his various wives and concubines. He had twenty sons by his wives and one daughter by the name of Tamar. He also had additional sons and daughters by his concubines. He loved his children profoundly. However, in his role as father he is shown to be apathetic; he should have been more proactive in advising and correcting his children, in family relationships and in love for one another.

David, had an agonizing experience in fatherhood with his and Bathsheba's firstborn son. Bathsheba, the wife of Uriah, and King David had an adulterous affair, which began when he observed her bathing on the roof. He saw this beautiful woman and lusted uncontrollably after her. "But I say to you that whoever looks at a woman to lust for her has already committed adultery with her in his heart" (Matthew 5:28). Bathsheba's husband was away at war and there was no one to protect her or defend her when King David sent for her. The Bible does not specifically address if she willingly agreed to the sexual encounter to take place, or if she performed it out of obedience to authority.

David was told that Bathsheba was the wife of Uriah, which meant he automatically violated the seventh commandment, Thou Shalt Not Commit Adultery. David chose to ignore the Law of God; instead he executed diplomatic abuse of power as king. Bathsheba was a victim of the king's power and authority that he dominated.

When Bathsheba realized she was pregnant she notified David. She knew her husband had been away at war and that David was the only person who could be the father of her child. He immediately tried to get Uriah to come home from battle, to be intimate with Bathsheba. His objective was for the married couple to come together to cover up the pregnancy from the eyes of the people, that Uriah was the father of the child.

Uriah was told he needed to go home from the battlefield in anticipation of spending personal time with Bathsheba his wife. Uriah did not agree with the special treatment that was being given him, because he knew the other soldiers were on the battlefield in combat. He thought it was very disloyal for him to be enjoying his wife, Bathsheba, while the other soldiers were in the heat of battle being deprived of their wives, homes, families, and other pleasures of life. Uriah refused to be honored with such indulgences and would not go to his house to be with Bathsheba.

"So when they told David, saying, Uriah did not go down to his house, David said to Uriah, Did you not come from a journey? Why did you not go down to your house? And Uriah said to David, The ark and Israel and Judah are dwelling in tents, and my lord Joab and the servants of my lord are encamped in the open fields. Shall I then go to my house to eat and drink, and to lie with my wife? As you live, and as your soul lives, I will not do this thing" (II Samuel 11:10-11). David conversed with Uriah about his refusal to go home and be with his wife, Bathsheba, but Uriah remained steadfast in his decision not to have a moment of pleasure at the army's expense. Uriah was a dedicated man to the cause and he was considerate, and placed others before himself!

And it came to pass in the morning that King David wrote a letter, preparing to break the sixth commandment, Thou Shalt Not Kill. "And he wrote in the letter, saying, Set Uriah in the forefront of the hottest battle, and retreat from him, that he may be struck down and die" (II Samuel 11:15). Uriah's loyalty did not end when he was out of the presence of King David. Returning to the battlefield Uriah did not open the decree and read the order. He did not allow curiosity to overcome his integrity. A disloyal or a curious soldier might have opened the decree and read it, to provide entertainment for the journey. After reading the life sentence the unfaithful soldier might have very well defected, thinking to himself that his chances of survival would be greater with the known enemy rather than with an intimate viper. But Uriah unknowingly hand-delivered his death sentence to Joab the commander of the army.

Joab, commander of the army, obeyed the directives of King David, and Uriah, the husband of Bathsheba, lost his life in battle. When Bathsheba's mourning had ended for her husband Uriah the Hittite, King David married her. "When the wife of Uriah heard that Uriah her husband was dead, she mourned for her husband. And when her mourning was over, David sent and brought her to his house, and she became his wife and bore him a son. But the thing that David had done displeased the LORD" (II Samuel 11:26-27).

Bathsheba gave birth to the son David had fathered, and the baby became very sick. Now, Nathan the prophet had come to King David. God advised the prophet of David's sins and he was exposed. He repented of his sins to the LORD and the Lord forgave David. He then began to fast and pray for their son, believing that God might allow the child to live. He continued to cry out of his soul for the preservation of life for their son but on the seventh day the baby died.

"So David said to Nathan, "I have sinned against the LORD. And Nathan said to David, The LORD also has put away your sin; you shall not die. However, because by this deed you have given great occasion to the enemies of the LORD to blaspheme, the child also who is born to you shall surely die. Then Nathan departed to his house. And the LORD struck the child that Uriah's wife bore to David, and it became ill. David therefore pleaded with God for the child, and David fasted and went in and lay all night on the ground. So the elders of his house arose and went to him, to raise him up from the ground. But he would not, nor did he eat food with them. Then on the seventh day it came to pass that the child died. And the servants of David were afraid to tell him that the child died. For they said, Indeed, while the child was alive, we spoke to him, and he would not heed our voice. How can we tell him that the child is dead? He may do some harm! When David saw that his servants were whispering, David perceived that the child was dead. Therefore, David said to his servants, Is the child dead? And they said, He is dead. So David arose from the ground, washed and anointed himself, and changed his clothes; and he went into the house of the LORD and worshiped. Then he went to his own house; and when he requested, they set food before him, and he ate. Then his servants said to him, What is this that you have done? You fasted and wept for the child while he was alive, but when the child died, you arose and ate food. And he said, While the child was alive, I fasted and wept; for I said, Who can tell whether the LORD will be gracious to me, that the child may live? But now he is dead; why should I fast? Can I bring him back again? I shall go to him, but he shall not return to me" (II Samuel 12:13-23).

It is so refreshing to know and realize that the mercies God has for His children are unmatched. David, a man after His own heart, had sinned against the LORD. He had disobeyed God's commandments by allowing the lust of the flesh to entice him to commit adultery with Uriah's wife. This sin eventually led to the death of Uriah. Nathan, the prophet told David that God had forgiven his sins: he prophesied to him that the child would certainly die.

According to the Law, David sins were punishable by death, the LORD forgave David of his sins. The death of the child was a horrible pain of the consequence of David's sin. David and Bathsheba were very hurt by the loss of their child. David had the type of relationship with the LORD that he felt he could move God through fasting, prayer, weeping, worship, and tears. God, being sovereign in power and majesty, struck the child and he died on the seventh day.

David and Bathsheba grieved the traumatic loss of their son. It is not the natural order for a child to die before the parents. Naturally one would anticipate the death of the older individual before the death of the younger. The death of a loved one is hard for most people but the death of a child is almost more than a parent can bear. David knew and recognized that the sin of adultery, murder, among others, had led to the death of his son. The penalty of sin was already covered; the prophet, Nathan, plainly told David that the LORD had forgiven him and that he would not die and his sins had been completely forgiven. "For the wages of sin is death, but the gift of God is eternal life in Christ Jesus our Lord" (Romans 6:23). The baby's death was not a punishment or penalty for the sins of David, a man after God's own heart!

David demonstrated godly repentance during his fasting, weeping, and praying while the baby was alive. He used this time to turn his attention and intimacy back to the God of Israel, the One he was very familiar with. Storms and hardships in our daily lives will often bring us back into perfect alignment with our Father. David in his kingly glory and majesty had become too complacent in the palace, living in luxury and comfort. "It happened in the spring of the year, at the time when kings go out to battle, that David sent Joab and his servants with him, and all Israel; and they destroyed the people of Ammon and besieged Rabbah. But David remained at Jerusalem" (II Samuel 11:1).

During this time of idleness and not walking in purpose and leadership, he found himself in the grip of a lustful spirit, pursuing another man's wife. "You shall not covet your neighbor's house; you shall not covet your neighbor's wife, nor his male servant, nor his female servant, nor his ox, nor his donkey, nor anything, that is your neighbor's" (Exodus 20:17). David was in the process of breaking the tenth commandment of Yahweh when he made plans to take Uriah the Hittite's wife.

David was quick to ask God to forgive his sins when the prophet Nathan gave him a summary of the poor man and his one ewe lamb, and how he was violated by the rich man. He became angry and compassionate about the plight of the victim, going so far as to tell Nathan that the person who committed such an offense is worthy of death. He had quickly forgotten that he had broken the sixth, seventh, and tenth commandments. Mankind can easily recognize the faults in others before they realize the sin in themselves. "Hypocrite! First remove the plank from your own eye, and then you will see clearly to remove the speck from your brother's eye" (Matthew 7:5). How many of us are guilty of peeping into our neighbor's mini storage, before taking inventory of our own warehouse? Is your storage empty and debris-free, before using the magnifying glass on others?

"Then one of them, a lawyer, asked Him a question, testing Him, and saying. Teacher, which is the great commandment in the law? Jesus said to him, You shall love the LORD your God with all your heart, with all your soul, and with all your mind. This is the first and great commandment. And the second is like it: You shall love your neighbor as yourself. On these two commandments hang all the Law and the Prophets" (Matthew 22:35-40). Jesus made it very plain when he gave the lawyer this dynamic answer to his frivolous question. If one could visualize two bookends, the first bookend reads "Thou shalt love the LORD thy God with all thy heart, and with all thy soul, and with all thy mind." The second bookend reads "Thou shalt love thy neighbor as thyself." One can clearly see that the other commandments would fall amid the first and second bookends. The other commandments are not going around, over, or through them, they are simply going between them. If King David or any of God's children concentrated on these two commandments they can truly be victorious and be overcomers in their spiritual walk. When we observe these two commandments the remaining eight are enclosed as a bonus. In other words, they should be effortless, and they should fit right in.

Generalizing, the Ten Commandments is dealing with the love of God and the love toward our fellow man. The first four commandments detail how God wants to be treated and the remaining six let us know how He wants man to treat each other. God is so full of love and of kindness toward His creation. He gave mankind a choice: we can either accept Him or reject Him. This freedom to choose really lets one know that God is OMNIPOTENT. Individuals who have power struggles tend to inflict demands on others to make themselves feel superior.

Yahweh, who is strong and mighty in power, gives every man a free will. In exercising our free will there is accountability to a sovereign God. Free will can be looked at in this aspect, an individual might purchase a gun to be used for protection from assaults and crimes, and may have a license to carry the weapon. Because a person is authorized to possess the weapon, it does not mean it can be used to wreak havoc at the owner's discretion. There are civil and spiritual laws that must be enforced and respected. We have been chosen to choose!!! God is our sovereign Father in our lives! "I call heaven and earth as witnesses today against you, that I have set before you life and death, blessing and cursing; therefore choose life, that both you and your descendants may live;" (Deuteronomy 30:19). God has given man the liberty to choose, His preferred choice for us, is life. Will you accept the nudging? Will your choice be life or death? Will your choice be Heaven or Hell?

David was blessed with many children before and after the death of the son he fathered with Bathsheba. He went unto Bathsheba, his wife, after their son's death when the time was appropriate, and she conceived and a son named Solomon was born to their union. "Then David comforted Bathsheba his wife, and went in to her and lay with her. So she bore a son, and he called his name Solomon. Now the Lord loved him, and He sent word by the hand of Nathan the prophet: So he called his name Jedidiah, because of the LORD" (II Samuel 12:24-25). As stated before; David loved all his sons and daughters. He also fathered two stunningly beautiful children by his wife Maacah. The son's name was Absalom and the daughter's name was Tamar. Both these children possessed remarkable physical attractions. David's firstborn son was Ammon by his wife Abinoam. Tamar was so beautiful that her brother Amnon, their father's oldest son, began to lust after his young sister.

By birth order, Ammon was the next in line to the throne of David. Amnon was much older than his sister Tamar who was still a young virgin residing in her father's house. His love for Tamar, was unnatural and unhealthy; it was far different from how a brother should love his younger sister. He allowed his feelings of desire and lust to take root and grow into something very polluting. "After this Absalom the son of David had a lovely sister, whose name was Tamar; and Amnon the son of David loved her.

Amnon was so distressed over his sister Tamar that he became sick; for she was a virgin. And it was improper for Amnon to do anything to her" (II Samuel 13:1-2).

As an heir to the throne of David, Amnon could have had any of the young, beautiful virgins in Israel who were not his sister. But his obsession for Tamar drove his thoughts into paths of unrighteousness. Causing his sin-penetrated mind to operate in the dark and fleshly realm. He was receptive to the ungodly counsel he received and he made no attempt to stray from the devious plan!

"But Amnon had a friend whose name was Jonadab the son of Shimeah, David's brother. Now Jonadab was a very crafty man. And he said to him, Why are you, the king's son, becoming thinner day after day? Will you not tell me? Amnon said to him, I love Tamar, my brother Absalom's sister. So Jonadab said to him, Lie down on your bed and pretend to be ill. And when your father comes to see you, say to him, Please let my sister Tamar come and give me food, and prepare the food in my sight, that I may see it and eat it from her hand" (II Samuel 13:3-5). Let it be noted that Jonadab, Amnon's friend and counsel, was a close cousin on his father's side who helped him devise and carry out this wicked action. Jonadab had his mischievous eye on the heir to the throne and over time observed Amnon in a state of distress.

It's very alarming to see how calmly and innocently Amnon put forth his description of Tamar to Jonadab. Suddenly, Tamar is only Absalom's sister not Amnon's; but Absalom remains his brother. It appears that sin can delete and rearrange DNA to gratify its selfish ambitions. Tamar was just as much Amnon's sister as Absalom was his brother. The enemy will allow you to rearrange your loyalties and obligations in your heart to satisfy sin. Prior to sin manifesting, the thing or things are rehearsed in your mind. Jonadab, is not guiltless of plotting against Tamar, who was his virgin first cousin. He may have had a hidden lust agenda toward Tamar also; he was too quick to come up with a naughty plan to line up for his cousin Amnon to execute.

"Then Amnon lay down and pretended to be ill; and when the king came to see him, Amnon said to the king, Please let Tamar my sister come and make a couple of cakes for me in my sight, that I may eat from her hand. And David sent home to Tamar, saying, Now go to your brother Amnon's house, and prepare food for him. So Tamar went to her brother Amnon's house, and he was lying down. Then she took flour and kneaded it, made cakes in his sight, and baked the cakes. And she took the pan and placed them out before him, but he refused to eat. Then Amnon said, Have everyone go out from me. And they all went out from him" (II Samuel 13:6-9). King David was a very weak father concerning his children. His love and desire to please and comfort his children in various situations outweighed his wisdom, sound judgment, and decision making.

The first thing David should have done when he came to see Amnon was to have him examined by the palace physician. Surely, one was on staff and available to check him out thoroughly. If it was truly cakes that he longed for in his feigned state of illness, the palace cooks could have made cakes that could have won a blue ribbon or the top prize for baking. King David's thoughts might have momentarily dwelt on the sick son Bathsheba and he had, who died. He was probably moved with deep compassion. He sent for his daughter Tamar to honor his son's request. Tamar, being an obedient daughter and a loving sister, did not refuse to obey her father's or brother's request. Tamar probably considered it an honor to be called upon to serve.

When Tamar had prepared the meal for Amnon she attempted to serve him, only to have him follow through with his evil plan. "Then Amnon said to

Tamar, Bring the food into the bedroom, that I may eat from your hand. And Tamar took the cakes which she had made, and brought them to Amnon her brother in the bedroom" (II Samuel 13:10). He wanted intimate interaction with Tamar his sister, much more than he wanted his necessary food. A lying and seducing spirit was grappling Amnon and his members.

"Now when she had brought them to him to eat, he took hold of her and said to her, Come lie with me, my sister. But she answered him, No, my brother do not force me, for no such thing should be done in Israel. Do not do this disgraceful thing! And I, where could I take my shame? And as for you, you would be like one of the fools in Israel. Now therefore, please speak to the king; for he will not withhold me from you. However, he would not heed her voice; and being stronger than she, he forced her and lay with her" (II Samuel 13:11-14).

Throughout all the confusion and trickery Amnon remembers even in his state of stupidity that Tamar is his sister. Even so, he asks her to lie with him; it's all about a selfish Amnon and what he wants. Tamar in her wisdom warns her brother to rethink his decision and begs him not to force such an atrocious act upon her. She knew if he went to their father and requested her for his wife their father the king would have given her to Amnon in marriage. But her pleading with him was to no avail.

Tamar to the best of her ability tried earnestly to convince her brother not to bring shame on her life by committing rape. She knew she would merely exist with the stigma of rape being on her for life. Tamar tried to think about how he would be viewed as a fool by the Israelites, but he did not listen to what Tamar tried to tell him about the outcome of his sin. Amnon wanted to enjoy sin for a season without thinking about the effects it would have on him, his sister, and their family. His physical strength and inhumanity forced itself upon the weaker vessel Tamar, and he raped his virgin sister!

"Then Ammon hated her exceedingly, so that the hatred with which he hated her was greater than the love with which he had loved her. And Amnon said to her, Arise, be gone! So she said to him, No, indeed! This evil of sending me away is worse than the other that you did to me, But he would not listen to her. Then he called his servant who attended him and said, Here! Put this woman out, away from me, and bolt the door behind her" (II Samuel 13:15-17). Isn't life strange? The very person Amnon thought he loved and lusted after, he immediately began to hate once the trespass was completed. He wanted Tamar to remove herself from his sight; if he had been proactive and listened to her pleas earlier this devastation could have been avoided. Tamar did not move away from the scene of the crime swiftly enough for him, so he requested the very men he had put out of the room to now come and, not only to put his violated sister out, but also to lock the door behind her. Immediately, Amnon feels he needs to be protected from Tamar by locking the door.

A locked door does not erase the shame, disgrace, sin, or guilt that has happened behind closed doors. If he had been insistent about the locked-door policy earlier, he should have locked himself away from bringing shame and hurt to his virgin sister. This was a violation of Tamar's right as a human being. He behaved as though he were a mindless dog in heat, to do such ruination toward Tamar. How many of us would be so selfish as to destroy an innocent life, and to destroy one with a virtuous character, to fulfill a lustful, or euphoric thrill?

"Now she had on a robe of many colors, for the king's virgin daughters wore such apparel. And his servant put her out and bolted the door behind her. Then Tamar put ashes on her head, and tore her robe of many colors that was on her, and laid her hand on her head and went away crying bitterly" (II Samuel 13:18-19). When Tamar came in to serve her supposedly sick brother she was wearing a garment that signified who she was. The robe signified she was a virgin daughter of the king. Amnon ignored her robe of many colors and what it stood for; he made it black with sin and pollution by abusing her right to remain a virgin. The ashes Tamar placed on her head after her brother raped her was a sign of mourning for the dead, among ancient Hebrews. I believe Tamar was mourning twofold: first for herself, that she was raped and was cast out like a dead dog, and second for Amnon, knowing that death was an inevitable fate for him for such an offense.

"And Absalom her brother said to her, Has Amnon your brother been with you? But now hold your peace, my sister. He is your brother; do not take this thing to heart. So Tamar remained desolate in her brother Absalom's house. But when King David heard of all these things, he was very angry. And Absalom spoke to his brother Amnon neither good nor bad. For Absalom hated Amnon, because he had forced his sister Tamar" (II Samuel 13:20-22). When Absalom confronted Tamar and asked her if Amnon had raped her, he advised her to be silent about the terrible offense her brother had committed. Where were the rights of the virgin daughter of the king in the eyes of Absalom? Absalom protected Tamar and had her come to his house where she remained unmarried.

King David was quite upset when he heard the sad news about Tamar, but the Bible does not mention whether he acted against the rapist. Similarly, David took no action in the rape of Bathsheba, Uriah's wife, at the time, until he was briefed by the prophet Nathan. "keeping mercy for thousands, forgiving iniquity and transgression and sin, by no means clearing the guilty, visiting the iniquity of the fathers upon the children and the children's children to the third and the fourth generation" (Exodus 34:7). God forgives the penalty of sin when one repents, yet the consequences of sin must be dealt with, even generationally.

When a child urinates on the bedding the parent forgives the child and possibly suggests that the child try to get up and use the bathroom. The bed-wetting incident is forgiven; however, the consequences are going to have to be dealt with. The sheets need to be washed and the mattress sanitized. The child needs to be bathed and dried, clean clothes need to be put on. In other words when sin is committed, the consequences do not disappear into oblivion!

Absalom continued to move inwardly and outwardly throughout the palace, going through life as if nothing had happened to his sister Tamar. He waited for two years to attempt a planned revenge against Amnon his brother, the rapist. Imagine Absalom keeping hatred in check so that those who were around him did not have a clue that a battle would ensue. In public, he was a successor to the throne who displayed strong leadership qualities, and one whom the people grew to love and admire. In private he had to face the shame and disgrace that was forced on his sister Tamar by their self-centered brother Amnon.

In private the mask could be removed, and the situation grew critically day by day, month by month and year by year. As Amnon moved around without a stigma or mark of the offensive crime he had inflicted on Tamar, she was living a life of abandonment and distress. I can only imagine how Tamar the injured virgin felt about herself after her father would not step up to the throne and punish sin in the palace. To have a king who as a father allowed such devastation to come upon his young, impressionable, virgin daughter and did nothing is a catastrophe!

"And it came to pass, after two full years, that Absalom had sheepshearers in Baal Hazor, which is near Ephraim; so Absalom invited all the king's sons. Then Absalom came to the king and said, Kindly note, your servant has sheepshearers; please, let the king and his servants go with your servant. But the king said to Absalom, No, my son, let us not all go now, lest we be a burden to you. Then he urged him, but he would not go; and he blessed him. Then Absalom said, If not, please let my brother Amnon go with us. And the king said to him, Why should he go with you? But Absalom urged him; so he let Amnon and all the king's sons go with him" (II Samuel 13:22-27).

Absalom carried extreme detestation in his heart against Amnon, and his hatred was great. Brotherly love had absolutely no place in Absalom's heart. He treasured his sister who had been sexually assaulted by Amnon their half-brother. Absalom's hidden agenda was soon to be revealed to everyone. He wanted to get rid of Amnon for multiple reasons:

1. *for the sex crime against Tamar and his bold disrespect in remaining visible after this atrocious act,*
2. *for the firstborn rights which included heirship to the throne, and*
3. *because their father King David did*

nothing to rebuke Amnon and make him accountable for his actions.

Absalom set about making sure that Amnon would not escape punishment for his evil deed.

"Now Absalom had commanded his servants, saying, Watch now, when Amnon's heart is merry with wine, and when I say to you, Strike Amnon! Then kill him. Do not be afraid. Have I not commanded you? Be courageous and valiant. So, the servants of Absalom did to Amnon as Absalom had commanded. Then all the king's sons arose, and each one got on his mule and fled. And it came to pass, while they were on the way, that news came to David, saying, Absalom has killed all the king's sons, and not one is left! So the king arose and tore his garments and lay on the ground, and all his servants stood by with their clothes torn" (II Samuel 13:28-31). Absalom had assured his servants not to be fearful in carrying out the murder plot, and urged them to be courageous. Even though he knew that killing his brother would not be a good thing for King David his father, Absalom at this point did not care. Amnon was massacred. When the news came to King David that all his sons were dead, he and his servants immediately went into mourning.

"Then Jonadab the son of Shimeah, David's brother; answered and said, Let not my lord suppose they have killed all the young men, the king's sons, for only Amnon is dead. For by the command of Absalom this has been determined from the day that he forced his sister Tamar. Now therefore, let not my lord the king take the thing to his heart, to think that all the king's sons are dead. For only Amnon is dead" (II Samuel 13:32-33). Jonadab, the demon-influenced nephew of King David, was now before the king pretending to be a Balm in Gilead. Jonadab had been instrumental in Amnon's action earlier, the wicked but perfect scenario for the rape of his cousin Tamar. Polluted Jonadab then revealed to his uncle the king that he had been privy to the premeditated murder of Amnon, even while not saying so. In other words, Jonadab believed that Amnon's death at the hands of Absalom was inevitable!

How dare Jonadab formulate the words in his mouth to tell King David not to take this thing to heart! Whether King David lost all his sons or only one, it was still a sibling murder, and the loss of his child at the hand of another child was a calamity. Tragedy in its most crafty form had just been manifested at the hands of evildoers. Jonadab was telling King David that Amnon the perpetrator, the only one who forced himself on the virgin Tamar, was now justifiably murdered. Not once did he tell the king it was his brilliant idea to plan the whole thing out from start to finish. If the truth had been known and justice fully extended for the sexual abuse of Tamar, would Jonadab be dead as well since he was a co-conspirator?

"So Absalom fled and went to Geshur, and was there three years. And King David longed to go to Absalom. For he had been comforted concerning Amnon, because he was dead" (II Samuel 13:38-39). David mourned the death of his firstborn son Amnon, just as he had mourned the death of the son he conceived with Uriah's wife. David was a father who loved his children passionately and tenderly. Amnon was a son who was heir to the royal line. As malicious as he and Absalom proved to be, their father loved them unconditionally. Our heavenly Father has this same type of love for His children. King David's love for his son Absalom made him long to see him, despite the treacherous act he had committed. However, King David's longing is not strong enough for him to send for Absalom to come.

Absalom eventually could return to Jerusalem from Geshur after his exile. King David let him return to his former house, but did not allow him to see him.

Absalom was near the king, yet so far. The two of them were separated by the royal choice of King David. Not liking the separation, Absalom continued to call for Joab the captain of the army to arrange a meeting between the two of them, but Joab ignored his requests. After becoming upset with Joab because he would not connect him to the king when he asked, Absalom had his servants burn Joab's barley fields. This cruel act got the attention of Joab and he went to see Absalom.

"And Absalom answered Joab, Look, I sent to you, saying, Come here, so that I may send you to the king, to say, Why have I come from Geshur? It would be better for me to be there still. Now therefore, let me see the king's face; but if there is iniquity in me, let him execute me. So Joab went to the king and told him. And when he had called for Absalom, he came to the king and bowed himself on his face to the ground before the king. Then the king kissed Absalom" (II Samuel 14:32-33).

Absalom was a strong-willed, power-driven individual and what he wanted was to manipulate the love his father had for him, to achieve success dishonestly! How many of us navigate through relationships with hidden agendas to acquire selfish ambitions or goals?

5

DAVID: AS A WARRIOR/KING

DAVID'S VICTORY over Goliath when he was a mere youngster was only the beginning of his success as a warrior. In a few years, David became the King of Judah in the southern kingdom, and Ish-bosheth, the fourth son of King Saul, was king of Israel in the northern kingdom. "And the king and his men went to Jerusalem against the Jebusites, the inhabitants of the land, who spoke to David, saying, You shall not come in here; but the blind and the lame will repel you, thinking, David cannot come in here" (II Samuel 5:6). David knew that because the city was so greatly fortified the handicapped were posted in charge of the city instead of the able-bodied. He and his soldiers seized the city and he reigned at that location, through the power and destiny of Yahweh.

"For by You I can run against a troop, By my God I can leap over a wall. As for God, His way is perfect; The word of the LORD is proven; He is a shield to all who trust in Him. For who is God, except the LORD? And who is a rock, except our God? It is God who arms me with strength, And makes my way perfect. He makes my feet like the feet of deer. And sets me on my high places. He teaches my hands to make war, So that my arms can bend a bow of bronze. You have also given me the shield of Your salvation; Your right hand has held me up, Your gentleness has made me great. You enlarged my path under me. So my feet did not slip. I have pursued my enemies and overtaken them: Neither did I turn back again till they were destroyed. I have wounded them, So that they could not rise; They have fallen under my feet. For You have armed me with strength for the battle; You have subdued under me those who rose up against me. You have also given me the necks of my enemies, So that I destroyed those who hated me" (Psalm 18:29-40).

David, with ease always gave Yahweh glory for the victories in his life. He acknowledged that it was only through the omnipotence of God that he and his troops could triumphantly fight against Jebus and conquer the city. Knowingly, he came against a fortified place, which, based on his natural or human ability and strength, could not possibly be breached. He fully recognized that he and his soldiers could not prevail or penetrate the wall without Yahweh's intervention. In this Psalm David thanks and praises Yahweh for being his armor. Victory and thanks fill his heart and mouth! When God win battles for us do we always, with smoothness and naturalness, give Him glory?

"They cried out, but there was none to save; Even to the LORD, but He did not answer them. Then I beat them as fine as the dust before the wind; I cast them out like dirt in the streets. You have delivered me from the strivings of the people; You have made me the head of the nations; A people I have not known shall serve me. As soon as they hear of me they obey me; The foreigners submit to me. The foreigners fade away, And come frightened from their hideouts. The LORD lives! Blessed be my Rock! Let the God of my salvation be exalted. It is God who avenges me, And subdues the peoples under me; He delivers me from my enemies. You also lift me up above those who rise against me; You have delivered me from the violent man. Therefore I will give thanks to You, O LORD, among the Gentiles, And sing praises to Your name. Great deliverance He gives to His king, And shows mercy to His anointed, To

David and his descendants forevermore" (Psalm 18:41-50).

The heathen had the audacity to cry out to David's God, but he answered them not a word. Yahweh, of the covenant told His children that they are the head and not the tail, above only and never beneath. David declared that strangers would submit in obedience when they heard of Him. He highly exalts Yahweh as his rock and deliverer. The heathen thought for a moment that they could defeat the LORD'S anointed; but they were put to utter shame. Victory Shall Be Ours!!!

Now king of the northern and southern kingdoms, David had more people to govern and more enemies to conquer. David was now setting up things in Jerusalem, the City of David, and was joyous and celebratory as he brought the Ark of the Covenant into its new home. "And so it was, when those bearing the ark of the LORD had gone six paces, that he sacrificed oxen and fatted sheep. Then David danced before the LORD with all his might; and David was wearing a linen ephod. So David and all the house of Israel brought up the ark of the LORD with shouting and with the sound of the trumpet. Now as the ark of the LORD came into the City of David, Michal, Saul's daughter, looked through a window and saw King David leaping and whirling before the LORD; and she despised him in her heart" (II Samuel 6:13-16).

Saul's daughter Michal, David's wife was watching him from a window as he danced intimately before the LORD. He danced so profoundly before the LORD and unto the LORD that he was exposed. Michal despised her husband in her heart, not publicly calling him out. Although Michal despised him inwardly for worshipping the LORD in the dance, it was manifested outwardly and David could very well discern that her heart was full of envy and contempt. "For nothing is secret that will not be revealed, nor anything hidden that will not be known and come to light" (Luke 8:17). Do we think for one moment, the things concerning others that we allow to fester in our hearts are not discerned by them and others spiritually?

"So they brought the ark of the LORD, and set it in its place in the midst of the tabernacle that David had erected for it. Then David offered burnt offerings and peace offerings before the LORD. And when David had finished offering burnt offerings and peace offerings, he blessed the people in the name of the LORD of hosts. Then he distributed among all the people, among the whole multitude of Israel, both the women and the men, to everyone a loaf of bread, a piece of meat, and a cake of raisins. So all the people departed, everyone to his house. Then David returned to bless his household. And Michal the daughter of Saul came to meet David, and said, How glorious was the king of Israel today in the eyes of the maids of his servants, as one of the base fellows shamelessly uncovers himself" (II Samuel 6:17-20)!

"For love is as strong as death, Jealousy as cruel as the grave; Its flame are flames of fire, A most vehement flame" (Song of Solomon 8:6b). Michal displayed a jealous attitude and mindset as she confronted the king about his dance of worship, praise, and celebration unto the LORD. Michal pointedly told her husband that he had uncovered himself before his servant's handmaids. After David completed the sacrifice to Yahweh he blessed the people with food and drinks in celebration. This type of sacrifice and worship reminds me of tithing and first fruit offering. Always give God His first, and the remainder will be blessed.

The enemy will use anyone, sometimes those closest, to grieve the Holy Spirit. While one is displaying love and worship to God, the enemy will send arrows of discouragement. Has anyone ever tried to block your praise and worship when you were at a culminating position in worship? Have you ever been in the thrust of praise or intimate worship, and you were interrupted or perhaps looked at with utter disgust? Not everyone is pleased when you are flooded with euphoria in total worship. Pure worship is almost absurd in the eyes of an inexperienced worshipper.

"So David said to Michal, It was before the LORD, who chose me instead of your father and all his house, to appoint me ruler over the people of the LORD, over Israel. Therefore I will play music before the LORD. And I will be even more undignified than this, and will be humble in my own sight. But as for the maidservants of whom you have spoken, by them I will be held in honor. Therefore Michal the daughter of Saul had no children to the day of her death" (II Samuel 6:21-23).

When the Ark of the Covenant was placed in its new home David sacrificed offerings to the LORD. After he completed the sacrifice to Yahweh he blessed the people with food to eat. Michal had a dilemma with her husband; she was probably unhappy about not having children. David had so many wives and concubines he perhaps could not come to her as often as she desired. Michal might have still resented him for removing her from the husband she had before her father King Saul's death.

Obviously, Michal's issue was that she could not separate a spiritual experience from a natural one. David was having a spiritual experience of worship in its purest form. If one has not known this level of worship, one can easily mistake it for sensual behavior. Satan got into Michal's heart because, he is unable to worship the LORD as in the past, he despised David and used someone close to him who had a crack in their spiritual foundation.

Michal kept graven images in her reach at her former home, where she used them to trick King Saul's soldiers into believing David was sick. Reflect again on "So Saul said, I will give her to him, that she may be a snare to him, and that the hand of the Philistines may be against him. Therefore Saul said to David a second time, You shall be my son-in-law today" (I Samuel 18:21a). Was Michal keeping idols in the City of David? Was Michal using idols as a pacifier for Yahweh's divine comfort and intimacy? Was the prophetic word "snare," used by her father, King Saul, being manifested?

David defeated the Philistines, the Ammonites, and Moab. Ruth, David's great-grandmother, was a native of Moab. He had left his parents and family in the Moabites' care, but they had been killed. The Moabites failed to properly care for his people as he had requested. David established his headquarters in Jerusalem, which is the capital city.

He strategically strove in military battles to secure land and receive booty for the treasury. After defeating various nations King David required that they pay tribute to his kingdom. As Yahweh blessed him to go in and out of battles safely throughout his administration, David realized the covenant God extended to him and his seed. Are we aware of the Blood Covenant extended through Yeshua Hamashiach (Jesus Christ The Messiah) to us and our seed?

DAVIDIC COVENANT

"Now therefore, thus shall you say to My servant David, Thus says the LORD of hosts: I took you from the sheepfold, from following the sheep, to be ruler over My people, over Israel. And I have been with you wherever you have gone, and have cut off all your enemies from before you, and have made you a great name, like the name of the great men who are on the earth. Moreover I will appoint a place for My people Israel, and will plant them, that they may dwell in a place of their own and move no more; nor shall the sons of wickedness oppress anymore, as previously, since the time that I commanded judges to be over My people Israel, and have caused you to rest from all your enemies. Also the LORD tells you that He will make you a house. When your days are fulfilled and you rest with your fathers, I will set up your seed after you, who will come from your body, and I will establish his kingdom. He shall build a house for My name, and I will establish the throne of his kingdom forever. I will be his Father, and he shall be My son. If he commits iniquity, I will chasten him with the rod of men and with the blows of the sons of men. But My mercy shall not depart from him, as I took it from Saul, whom I removed from before you. And your house and your kingdom shall be established forever before you. Your throne shall be established forever" (II Samuel 7:8-16). **David a man after God's own heart was chosen by Yahweh to receive a perpetual covenant!**

6

DAVID: AS A
WORSHIPPER/PSALMIST

WHEN ONE'S PERSONAL relationship with the Lord reaches an ultimate peak through obedience, honor, and love, a result of this union is true worship. David was intimate in worship with Yahweh. He had a keen passion for Yahweh and could express his feelings with ease through worship. I strongly believe this relationship began in his youth as a shepherd in the Judean hills taking care of his father Jesse's flock. His walk with the LORD was profound; it included the very essence of his being.

David's soul and spirit became synchronized with the Holy Spirit. The Holy Spirit is a Gentleman; He loves to be ministered to. During the earlier dispensation when the Holy Spirit would come upon mankind as Yahweh ordained. After the ascension of Christ and the day of Pentecost, the Holy Spirit dwells in the temple of believers.

David spent a great deal of time communing, and fellowshipping with Yahweh for his relationship to grow and expand. Worship can be accomplished through reading or reciting the Word of God orally, praying, singing, and so on, with the primary focus being toward God. If your spirit is attuned to the grace, forgiveness, peace, love, joy, beauty, and majesty of God, worship can be experienced in pure delight. David reached a dimension of holy ecstasy in Yahweh which stimulated him to go higher and higher in worship.

The Bible clearly depicts King David as a worshipper. The heart is the womb of our worship; it is the neonatal center for our worship. The heart protects and molds our worship as we allow the Holy Spirit to have dominion over our very being. Just as important it is for an infant to have a neonatal environment that resembles the warmth, and intimacy that the mother and the infant have developed over time, so too must the heart of man have an optimum mindset toward our Father, as in a pre-incarnate realm, to honor Him in spirit and in truth.

"O LORD, our Lord, How excellent is Your name in all the earth, Who have set Your glory above the heavens! Out of the mouth of babes and nursing infants You have ordained strength, Because of Your enemies, That You may silence the enemy and the avenger. When I consider Your heavens, the work of Your fingers, The moon and the stars, which You have ordained, What is man that You are mindful of him, And the son of man that You visit him? For You have made him a little lower than the angels, And You have crowned him with glory and honor. You have made him to have dominion over the works of Your hands; You have put all things under his feet, All sheep and oxen – Even the beasts of the field, The birds of the air, And the fish of the sea That pass through the paths of the seas. O LORD, our Lord, How excellent is Your name in all the earth" (Psalm 8:1-9)!

Psalm 8, which is credited to David and was probably accompanied by the gittith, expresses awe at the grandeur of God. I totally agree with David on the Excellency of the name of God in all the earth. No matter the continent, the culture, the race, the nation, the belief system, the state of the economy, or the oil reserves, His name is excellent in every square foot, mile, acre, or geographic boundary endlessly! No matter how young or powerless one may be, God has ordained strength because of one's enemies. When

God declares a thing in the face of our enemies He supersedes our inabilities and projects His abilities. This is an awesome awakening to know that the avenger, the enemy of God, will be stilled. The desire to seek after and act out in violence and hatred will not be allowed, because God has provided strength that will allow the action to come to a halt.

When David meditated, worshipped, and considered the vastness of creation that could be seen with the eyes, he is filled with awe to imagine what could be so breathtaking and noticeable about man that he is a consideration in the brilliance of the mind of God. What is so unique about man that God even thinks about him? Man was handmade and molded by the fingers of God, only a little lower than the angels. "For You have made him a little lower than the angels, And You have crowned him with glory and honor" (Psalm 8:5).

God has crowned man with glory and honor, hallelujah Jesus! This psalm reminds me of when I was a little girl, I loved to play with paper dolls. I could dress them any way that I wanted, and it was my decision if the paper doll would portray Raggedy Ann or the Queen of England. "You are worthy, O Lord, To receive glory and honor and power; For You created all things, And by Your will they exist and were created" (Revelation 4:11). In the Book of Revelation, it is clearly stated that all things were created for His pleasure. Are we pleased to honor, obey and glorify the Father, Son, and Holy Spirit, knowing we are created for that purpose?

Our Heavenly Father gave man dominion over His creations and placed all things under his feet, not for man to trip, stumble, or fall. However, mankind lost dominion temporarily with the first Adam. Mankind regained dominion through the shed blood of Jesus, the second Adam. Jesus of Nazareth was crucified, went to Hades, and was resurrected. He took captivity captive, and He ascended to Heaven to be seated at the right hand of Majesty. Glory and honor belongs to the Father for His plan of redemption! Blessings to Yeshua HaMashiach and the Holy Spirit! Hallelujah!!!

In Psalm 8, one can readily see the spirit of worship surrounding this work. David wore many hats during his lifetime; the hat of a worshipper properly fits on his head and complements him well. He glorified and exalted God in this Psalm, which is equivalent to worship. "LORD, who may abide in Your tabernacle? Who may dwell in Your holy hill? He who walks uprightly, And works righteousness, And speaks the truth in his heart; He who does not backbite with his tongue, Nor does evil to his neighbor, Nor does he take up a reproach against his friend; In whose eyes a vile person is despised, But he honors those who fear the LORD; He who swears to his own hurt and does not change; he who does not put out his money at usury, Nor does he take a bribe against the innocent. He who does these things shall never be moved" (Psalm 15:1-5). This Psalm is written by David describing a citizen of Zion.

Psalm 15 begins with a question; the operative word in the first verse is WHO? While meditating on "Who shall abide in thy tabernacle? Who shall dwell in thy holy hill?" I also consider an additional question, which is "Who is worthy?" David questioned God and furnished the answers as quickly as he asked the questions. We oftentimes ask the question nonchalantly and afterward the answer immediately presents itself. David acknowledged that God is holy, and He would do things that were right and honest. David also added that he refrained from talking about others, doing bad things to others, or criticizing his neighbor.

So, everyone must decide: to look wrong in the face and to declare it wrong. [[*Respect and honor those who walk in reverence unto God. Whoever, despite the outcome of speaking the truth will speak it without swaying. He that has money to loan will lend and will not exact a fee or interest on the loan. He who refuses to accept money or favor; to destroy someone who is innocent. When these specifications are clearly met and adhered to, you are seeing the citizen of Zion.*]] David is such an anointed and brilliant Psalmist! I give God the glory for allowing David's life and creative works to be read by mankind. Do you want to dwell in the city of Zion?

David took time to celebrate and fellowship with Yahweh. His prayers and devotions were offered up to Yahweh in perfect praise and worship. David was called by Yahweh "a man after God's own heart." When reading and meditating on his songs and poetry in the book of Psalms one can easily see why God refers to him in that way. David's life is the epitome of his Psalms. What is inside of you when you write or compose will flow with smoothness outwardly. What are you storing on the inside for God and others to see? Things that will bring honor or dishonor?

"The LORD is my light and my salvation; Whom shall I fear? The LORD is the strength of my life; Of whom shall I be afraid? When the wicked came against me To eat up my flesh, My enemies and foes, They stumbled and fell. Though an army may encamp against me, My heart shall not fear; Though war may rise against me, In this I will be confident. One thing I have desired of the LORD, That will I seek: That I may dwell in the house of the LORD All the days of my life, To behold the beauty of the LORD, And to inquire in His temple. For in the time of trouble He shall hide me in His pavilion; In the secret place of His tabernacle He shall hide me; He shall set me high upon a rock. And now my head shall be lifted up above my enemies all around me; Therefore I will offer sacrifices of joy in His tabernacle; I will sing, yes, I will sing praises to the LORD" (Psalm 27:1-6). This is a beautiful Psalm credited to David.

In the opening verse of Psalm 27, David declares that he is not afraid since the LORD is his light and salvation. In the same way, when there are times in our lives that dark drama and issues emerges, we should not fear because we are spiritually connected to the Light of the World. When the LORD is your salvation you can totally trust and depend on Him for divine protection. David reveals that the LORD is his strength; he fully realized when he fought the lion, the bear, and the armies, that Yahweh allowed him to defeat them. It was only the LORD'S strength that won the battles. Since he knew Yahweh to be omnipotent, he was not afraid in battle or conflict.

He clearly saw the hand of the LORD, and when his enemies attempted to end his life prematurely through trickery and game, they could not touch him. It did not move him, that innumerable forces came out in battle array. He was confident not in the visible host, but in the invisible host of the LORD. David, might have been in the middle of raging wars; but his desire was to be in the Tabernacle of the LORD. He was determined to be in the presence of the LORD and enjoy His beauty, and not in the drama on the battlefield.

He worshipped the LORD so intensely that he recognized that the pivotal place of safety was off limit to sinners, enemies, and those who transgressed the way of the LORD; it was so high on the top of the rock that it could not be reached by human means. David understood when he attained this position of elevation that there was divine safety. He chose to praise and worship the LORD MOST HIGH!!! In the Tabernacle, David offered sacrifices of joy and love, not sacrifices of rams and bullocks! Wow, what an overwhelming sacrifice unto the LORD! What sacrifice have you given to the LORD lately?

"Hear, O LORD, when I cry with my voice! Have mercy also upon me, and answer me. When You said, Seek My face, My heart said to You, Your face, LORD, I will seek. Do not hide Your face from me; Do not turn Your servant away in anger; You have been my help; Do not leave me nor forsake me, O God of my salvation. When my father and my mother forsake me, Then the LORD will take care of me. Teach me Your way, O LORD, And lead me in a smooth path, because of my enemies. Do not deliver me to the will of my adversaries; For false witnesses have risen against me, And such as breathe out violence. I would have lost heart, unless I had believed That I would see the goodness of the Lord In the land of the living. Wait on the LORD; Be of good courage, And He shall strengthen your heart; Wait, I say, on the LORD" (Psalm 27: 7-14)!

In Psalm 27:7-14, David is beseeching Yahweh to hear him when he cries unto Him. A mother is alerted when her baby cries. It doesn't matter how many babies are crying at the same time, the mother is immediately alerted to the cry of her baby. The cry of a baby can go on for a long time, but the compassion and mercy the mother has toward her baby allows her to soothe the baby, either by giving the baby a pacifier, a bottle, changing a diaper, bathing, or giving the baby hugs and kisses. In the same way, David wants the LORD to have mercy on him and answer him.

When the LORD said "Seek my face," David's mind and heart were eager to seek the face of the LORD. David does not want the LORD to hide his face far from him. He desires the LORD to be near him. When Moses met the LORD on Mount Sinai, the LORD covered Moses's face and put him in a cleft of the rock so he would not be able to see His face. David does not want Yahweh to put him away in anger, he wants the assurance of Yahweh's love and assistance to always be at his disposal. If his parents forsake him he wants the LORD to take him up.

I was thinking, when a small child's parents leave them prematurely, permanently, or temporarily there is a void — that child is vulnerable to the open arms of another person. Just to have someone to lift them up and comfort them in their trial or grief means so much. David wanted the LORD to teach him His statutes and lead him so that he would not be tripped up by his enemies. He does not want to be turned over to his enemies because they have gathered together lying witnesses against him.

Things in life sometimes are so traumatic that they squeeze the breath out of one. By faith David chose to believe to see the goodness of the LORD in the land. In today's world this psalm helps us cope with tsunamis, earthquakes, floods, hurricanes, volcanic eruptions, terrorism, high gasoline prices, unemployment, foreclosures, repossessions, bankruptcies, high divorce rate in the church, clergy falling into sin traps, church resembling the world, nations against nations, lawlessness, gang-banging, bombings, disobedient children, sexual predators, drugs, same-sex marriage, adultery, theft, fornication, sex traffic, human smuggling, inflation, stock market crashes, abounding sin, suicide, bullying, and other perversions. What a powerful Psalm! David is encouraging us. Are you as confident as David during these perilous times?

David has authored so many beautiful psalms it is hard to determine which one to expound on; they are all wonderful and powerful! One can sense the level of intimacy David had with Yahweh. In his writings, he is free to speak openly and unashamedly of his great love for his Creator. Even when David asks a question in the Psalms you can still feel the strength of his relationship with Yahweh. Questions you ask those with whom you are in a close relationship are very different from questions you would ask a stranger. The question or questions you would ask a stranger would have limitations. The questions you would ask of someone you know very well are unlimited.

The Book of Psalms reminds me of a diary, journal, or love letter to the one you love with all your heart, soul, and mind. In love, you release all of yourself to your mate; love reveals the uninhibited aspects of who you really are. Love allows you to uncover some things that perhaps in a different setting you would not have been afforded the freedom to do. Love and intimacy permit you to act unselfconsciously in the presence and the comfort of your mate. In love, you are not measured by perfection but by the motives and intents of your heart. Surely, one can clearly visualize why David was a man after God's own heart. Have you sent God a love letter of praise and worship recently?

"O LORD, You have searched me and known me. You know my sitting down and rising up; You understand my thought afar off. You comprehend my path and my lying down, And are acquainted with all my ways. For there is not a word on my tongue, But behold, O LORD, You know it altogether. You have hedged me behind and before, And laid Your hand upon me. Such knowledge is too wonderful for me; It is high, I cannot attain it. Where can I go from Your Spirit? Or where can I flee from Your presence? If I ascend into heaven, You are there; If I make my bed in hell, behold, You are there. If I take the wings of the morning, And dwell in the uttermost parts of the sea, Even there Your hand shall lead me, And your right hand shall hold me. If I say, Surely the darkness shall fall on me, Even the night shall be light about me; Indeed, the darkness shall not hide from You, But the night shines as the day; The darkness and the light are both alike to You. For You formed my inward parts; You covered me in my mother's womb. I will praise You, for I am fearfully and wonderfully made, Marvelous are Your works, And that my soul knows very well. My frame was not hidden from You, When I was made in secret, And skillfully wrought in the lowest parts of the earth. Your eyes saw my substance, being yet unformed. And in your book they all were written, The days fashioned for me, When as yet there were none of them. How precious also are Your thoughts to me, O God! How great is the sum of them! If I should count them, they would be more in number than the sand; When I awake, I am still with You. Oh, that You would slay the wicked, O God! Depart from me, therefore, you bloodthirsty men. For they speak against You wickedly; Your enemies take Your name in vain. Do I not hate them, O Lord, who hate You? And do I not loathe those who rise up against You? I hate them with perfect hatred; I count them my enemies. Search me, O God, and know my heart; Try me, and know my anxieties; And see if there is any wicked way in me, And lead me in the way everlasting" (Psalm 139:1-24).

Psalm 139 is written by David and bears the title "To the Chief Musician" or "To the Conqueror." God is so awesome! On September 11, 2001, the government in America decided to establish the TSA (Transportation Security Administration) in the aftermath of terrorism against our country. The Psalmist says God had searched him and known him. There is no electronic device that can begin to know or will ever know the depth of our being, but God knows everything. David declares that Yahweh knows when he sits and when he rises, his ups and downs. He did not have to give the LORD an account of his feelings or emotions, because God is omniscient (all knowing). He knows everything! Yahweh has precedence over the most sophisticated GPS (Global Positioning System). David knows that He surrounds his path and that He is familiar with all his ways. It matters not what direction David's mind, body or ways were shifted, God knows all and He is in all!

David proclaims that Yahweh knows the words on his tongue. Before the words are thought of or spoken it is known by the LORD. Just as a jeweler cleverly places a precious stone in position in a planned design, so has the Creator wrought His creation with His Designer's Touch. David is confessing Yahweh's knowledge is too wonderful, and too high for him.

Later, the prophet Isaiah was to agree: "For as the heavens are higher than the earth, So are My ways higher than your ways, And My thoughts than your thoughts" (Isaiah 55:9).

David asks a profound question, namely, where can he go from the LORD'S Spirit? To fully understand the question, we must remember how man was created: "And the LORD God formed man of the dust of the ground, and breathed into his nostrils the breath of life; and man became a living being" (Genesis 2:7). Because God breathed into man he is eternally connected, whether man chooses to act good, bad or indifferent. David understands this and answers his own question; he knows he can go no place that the LORD is not present. The LORD is omnipresent (everywhere at the same time).

David has concluded there is no place that he can go to get away from God's radar. If it is to the highest heaven, or to the lowest hell, or the deepest sea, Yahweh is there. Wherever David is he is assured that Yahweh's hand will lead and guide him. He is saying that the night and the light are the same to the LORD. Whether it is pitch-black night or the sunniest day, the LORD sees all! David affirms that it is the Creator who covered him before he was wrapped with the first external blanket or covering by his mother or midwife. Yahweh saw to every portion of his physical body being properly patterned in His likeness. The veins, blood, cells, muscles, bones, organs, and skin had to work on behalf of the assembly line of Heaven. He takes a praise break to exalt Yahweh for the unique qualities He has given to human development.

Before the first ultrasound was performed Yahweh knew the gender of the unborn child. That information may have not been given to his earthly parents, but the LORD knew. David shares that his substance was imperfect yet the LORD put all his members in His Book. The Holy Spirit would be upon David as he composed the Psalms. God completes in eternity before He begins in time. That is why Yahweh could tell Jeremiah the prophet, He knew him before he was formed in his mother's womb.

David is very confident about the punishment the LORD has for the wicked, and commands the wicked to depart out of his presence. He admits he hates what God hates. Finally, David wants Yahweh to search him and lead him in the way everlasting. The security checks and searches in airports and the metal detectors in schools, jails, courts, and other locations experience technical glitches sometimes. Due to human and technical breakdowns they may fail, but The Holy

One of Israel is able to search thoroughly and accurately and He is the Power Source that NEVER fails!

"Have mercy upon me, O God, According to Your lovingkindness; According to the multitude of Your tender mercies, Blot out my transgressions. Wash me thoroughly from my iniquity, And cleanse me from my sin. For I acknowledge my transgressions, And my sin is always before me. Against You, You only, have I sinned, And done this evil in Your sight — That You may be found just when You speak, And blameless when You judge. Behold, I was brought forth in iniquity, And in sin my mother conceived me. Behold, You desire truth in the inward parts, And in the hidden part You will make me to know wisdom. Purge me with hyssop, and I shall be clean; Wash me, and I shall be whiter than snow. Make me hear joy and gladness, That the bones You have broken may rejoice. Hide Your face from my sins, And blot out all my iniquities. Create in me a clean heart, O God, And renew a steadfast spirit within me. Do not cast me away from Your presence, And do not take Your Holy Spirit from me. Restore to me the joy of Your salvation, And uphold me by Your generous Spirit. Then I will teach transgressors Your ways, And sinners shall be converted to You. Deliver me from the guilt of bloodshed, O God, The God of my salvation, And my tongue shall sing aloud of Your righteousness. O Lord, open my lips, And my mouth shall show forth Your praise. For You do not desire sacrifice, or else I would give it; You do not delight in burnt offering. The sacrifices of God are a broken spirit, A broken and a contrite heart — These, O God, You will not despise. Do good in Your good pleasure to Zion; Build the walls of Jerusalem. Then You shall be pleased with the sacrifices of righteousness, With burnt offering and whole burnt offering; Then they shall offer bulls on Your altar" (Psalm 51:1-19).

Psalm 51 is a Psalm of David to the chief musician. This Psalm was birthed after Nathan the prophet came to him about Bathsheba. David's plea to Yahweh is, have mercy upon me. He realizes totally, after Nathan cleared up his blurred vision that he was the man who had committed adultery and murder. David recognized where he is spiritually and he immediately repents to the LORD for his sin and iniquity. In this psalm, he petitions Yahweh to have mercy upon him.

He could boldly ask Yahweh for mercy for he was in a covenant relationship with Him, and he is aware that one of His attributes is mercy. He knew the power, might, and sovereignty of the One whom he was making his request. He wanted the mercies of the

LORD to be extended to him; but most importantly he wanted his transgressions blotted out. David wanted his grotesque sin to be erased and removed permanently.

David desired a complete wash from his sin, not just a gentle rinse. When washing dirty clothes that are heavily soiled or stained, the rinse or gentle cycles are not sufficient. He wanted Yahweh to give his sin and iniquity a thorough and complete wash leaving no residue of his transgressions. David is in a mode to receive forgiveness for his exposed sin. He is aware of his sin against a Holy, Just, Righteous, and Forgiving God. David reflected on his forefather Adam and the original sin, knowing that he is in a fallen state and that he was covered in iniquity.

David wanted Yahweh to purge him with hyssop and purify him. He knew the priest used hyssop in the process of the cleansing of leper. The lepers, who were ceremoniously unclean until showing themselves to the priest after healing occurred. He saw himself symbolically as a leprous individual, laden with the filth of his sin and is now praying to Yahweh to make the sin offering for him. Sin will take one into deep, dark trenches, and only the light of the LORD can bring one from it grips. When the Holy Spirit shines the light of conviction upon you, will you stare at sin as an optical illusion or as a first-class ticket into the bowels of Hell? Simply, and prayerfully repent of all sin!

David, is seeking Yahweh with all his power and strength to deliver him of the iniquity and disease that has tormented his being. He wanted the restoration of His joy and peace to flood his soul, like he enjoyed before he leased out rooms at the Palace of Iniquity. The joy of adoring the fellowship and sweet communion of the LORD is what is needed most in his life.

David wanted Yahweh to instill the right spirit in him so he could continue in obedience, humility, and love with the LORD. He not only presents his intimate and private petitions to Yahweh; he also interceded for the people God had entrusted to his care. He was experienced enough in leadership to recognize what the leader does affects the whole. David was not selfish in his prayer; he wanted mercy to be extended to the people as well. He wanted a clean slate so they could all begin again.

I love to incorporate this psalm in my personal prayers. The 51st number of Psalm is so powerful, and I know it touches the very heart of Yahweh. Leaders, are you willing to pray for forgiveness for yourselves and to intercede for those God has given you? Are you ready for the Shekinah Glory of God to penetrate our sanctuaries worldwide?

In David's eagerness and willingness to grasp and not amend God's law, at every level of his life, we can learn to visualize why God saw him as "A man after His own heart." David's continuous exaltation of God as the Majestic King, past, present, and future is demonstrated through his life. This is another reason for God's affection and love for David.

The prophet Samuel anointed him with oil as the king of Israel, and he never lost sight of who the King of Kings of Israel and every nation is. David demonstrated that he was an instrument of praise and worship. Despite controversies, dilemmas, rejections, loss of family, sin, and other misfortunes, he refused to forfeit giving God true praise and worship; he worshipped the LORD in spirit and in truth. God looks at the heart and man looks at the outside. God could see past his human flaws and see his true being. We should have the same testimonies as David had, as instruments of praise and worship! When we are convicted of our sins and iniquities by the Holy Spirit, are we willing to quickly repent and began again? Are we willing to fully embrace His G.R.A.C.E (God's Restitution Authorizing Christs' Eminence)?

The biblical account of David's life lets us clearly

see that if we model ourselves with the character traits of obedience, humility, commitment, love, faith, repentance, praise and worship unto the Lord, each of us, too, will be **AN INSTRUMENT of HORN DIVINELY CALLED!!!**

POEM: IMAGE OF YOU

BY JOAN E. WATSON

In the image of God created He them,
A work of art, a majestic gem!
From Heaven's door He proudly stood,
To view His work and it was very good!
God's masterpieces are large, medium, and small,
Creatively He made them to stand short, average, or tall!
We are all sealed with His designer's signature.
The breath of life freely flowing so we can endure!
The image of God is the pure image of you,
Rejoice as you look in the mirror and esteem the view!

POEM: IMAGE OF YOU

This Poem Was Inspired by Psalm 139

I OFFER CHRIST TO YOU

If you believe that God gave His only son, the Lamb of God, to die for the sins of the world, and if you repent of your sin and believe that God raised Jesus Christ from the grave, you will be saved. He is waiting on you to come to Him in faith, submission and obedience, so He can give you eternal life with Him. Jesus Christ paid the full price for the penalty of sin and He is waiting on you to receive the gift of salvation! "that if you confess with your mouth the Lord Jesus and believe in your heart that God has raised Him from the dead, you will be saved. For with the heart one believes unto righteousness, and with the mouth confession is made unto salvation" (Romans 10:9-10). It is a GIFT! Come to Jesus and receive EVERYTHING!!!

On this _____ day of the _____ month of _____ in the year, I surrender All!

May your life be eternally changed, and to God be all the Glory!

In His Service,
Joan E. Watson

NOTES

CHAPTER 2: DAVID AN INSTRUMENT OF HORN

1. Instrument of Horn: A name prophetically given to me by God after a three-day fast in 2000. Horn denotes power. The shofar, (a ram's horn, trumpet), is often used as an instrument of spiritual warfare, to show strength. Instrument of Horn Ministries, a 501c3 organization, was birthed in 2002.

CHAPTER 3: DAVID: AS A FRIEND

2. One step and timing: This phrase is one that the Holy Spirit revealed to me several years ago, after fasting and prayer. Since then, it has served as a

reminder that God has a time and purpose for everything in our lives as He reveals His divine destiny for us.

ABOUT THE AUTHOR

Joan is most adamant concerning her walk with the Lord Jesus. She is totally committed to the call on her life. Quality time is spent in prayer and intercession, studying, meditating, and expounding on the Word of God, which is one her greatest passion. She is involved in ministry at her local church as a licensed evangelist missionary, she is on the Mother's Board, she is a teacher of the infallible Word of God, and she assists and serve in other areas where her Pastor, church, and leaders request.

She is a wife, mother, grandmother, godmother, aunt, niece, cousin, and friend to many. She really enjoys living a saved and joyous life in Christ. Joan enjoys people and doing fun things that interacts with others.

The safest place to be is in the will of God! Joan has a love for the nation of Israel! Remember to pray for the peace of Jerusalem. "Pray for the peace of Jerusalem: May they prosper who love you. Peace be within your walls, Prosperity within your palaces. For the sake of my brethren and companions, I will now say, Peace be within you. Because of the house of the LORD our God I will seek your good" (Psalm 122:6-9).

CONTACT JOAN E. WATSON

Write or E-mail:
Instrument of Horn Ministries
Attn: Joan E. Watson
P.O. Box 924203
Houston, Texas 77292

Email: instrumentofhornministries@sbcglobal.net
www.instrumentofhorn.org

JOIN MINISTRY IN THE WORD

INSTRUMENT OF HORN MINISTRIES

Dial: 712 770-4700
Access Code: 976290
First & Third Saturday of Each Month
7:00 a.m. CST

www.ingramcontent.com/pod-product-compliance
Lightning Source LLC
LaVergne TN
LVHW041630070426
835507LV00008B/532